The Wonder of
LOONS

The Wonder of
LOONS

Adapted from Tom Klein's *Loon Magic for Kids*
by Patricia Lantier-Sampon

Gareth Stevens Publishing
MILWAUKEE

For a free color catalog describing Gareth Stevens' list of high-quality books, call 1-800-341-3569 (USA) or 1-800-461-9120 (Canada).

Library of Congress Cataloging-in-Publication Data

Lantier-Sampon, Patricia.
  The wonder of loons / adapted from Tom Klein's Loon magic for kids by Patricia Lantier-Sampon.
    p. cm. — (Animal wonders)
  Includes index.
  Summary: Text and photographs introduce the shy water bird famous for its mournful call.
  ISBN 0-8368-0856-8
  1. Loons—Juvenile literature. [1. Loons.] I. Klein, Tom, 1947- Loon magic for kids. II. Title. III. Series.
QL696.G33L36   1992
59.4'42—dc20
                                                                        92-16945

North American edition first published in 1992 by
Gareth Stevens Publishing
1555 North RiverCenter Drive, Suite 201
Milwaukee, WI 53212, USA

This edition is abridged from *Loon Magic for Kids*, copyright © 1989 by NorthWord Press, Inc., and written by Tom Klein, first published in 1989 by NorthWord Press, Inc., and published in a library edition by Gareth Stevens, Inc. Additional end matter copyright © 1992 by Gareth Stevens, Inc.

Picture Credits:
Bob Baldwin 2, 14, 21, 40; Adam Bayer 38; Denver Bryan 38; R.C. Burke 4, 6; Daniel J. Cox 8, 19, 27, 42, 43; Glenn Irwin 24, 31; Edgar Jones 13, 29; Tom Klein 7, 26; S. Kraseman (DRK photo) 28; Tom Magelson (DRK photo) 20, 30; Tom Martinson (front cover); Peter Roberts 17, 30, 33, 37; W.E. Ruth 45; Lynn Rogers 18, 25, 34, 35, 39, (back cover); Tom Walker 12; Mark Wallner 23.

Cover design: Kristi Ludwig

Printed in the United States of America

  2 3 4 5 6 7 8 9 98 97 96 95 94 93

TABLE OF CONTENTS

Page

Loons are shy water
birds that live on
clean northern lakes.
The songs of the loons
are wild and strange.
Some people say the
birds are magical.

Loons spend most of their lives on water. Their long, thin bodies are specially *adapted* for this kind of living, and their long, pointed bills help them capture *prey*. Loons catch most of their fish by diving underwater. Sometimes they dive as deep as two hundred feet!

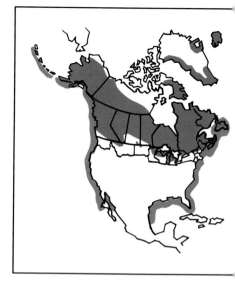

Common Loon

Loons spend the warmest months of each year on northern lakes and rivers. There the adults make nests and raise their chicks. When the weather gets cold in autumn, loon families *migrate* south to warm ocean coasts.

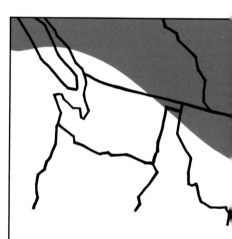

Detail of Common Loon breeding range

■ Wintering Range
■ Breeding Range

Red-throated Loon

Pacific Loon

Yellow-billed Loon

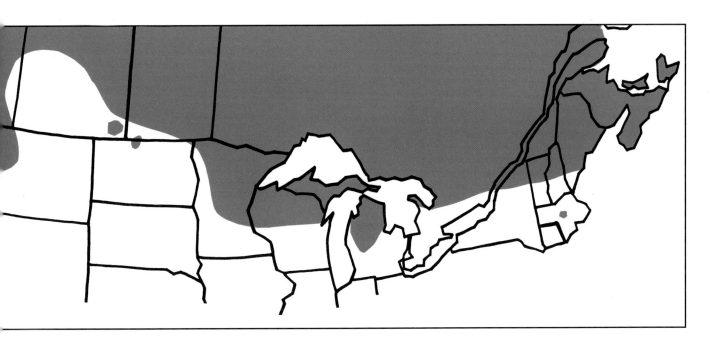

Four types of
loons live in
the U.S. and
Canada: the
red-throated
loon (left), the
yellow-billed
loon (top), the
Pacific loon
(bottom), and
the common
loon. These
birds are not
all the same
size or color.

Loons like privacy, so people should not get too close to their nests. The birds might fly away and never return!

The common loon is most often seen and heard by people who live near lakes. Both male and female common loons have black-and-white *plumage*. And both have bright red eyes that may help them see better when they fish underwater.

The common loon is famous for its mournful call. This lonesome sound has thrilled people for many years.

Loons often swim underwater with their eyes open in search of prey. After spotting a fish, the loons dive and try to catch it with their bills.

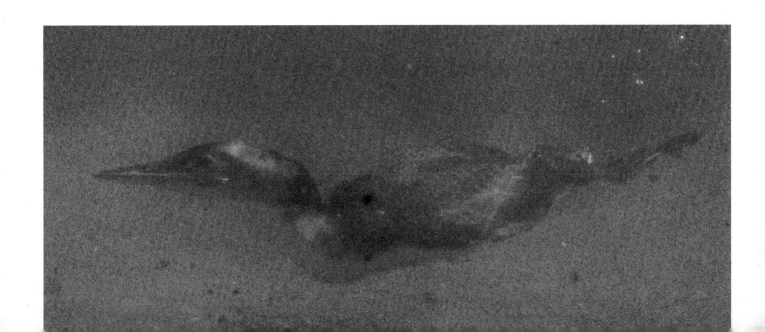

Loons bring the fish they catch back to the surface of the water. These birds do not chew their food. Because they have elastic throats, they can swallow food whole.

Loons eat small fish, frogs, crayfish, and leeches.

Loons have two special water dances. In one (left), the loons actually chase other birds away by walking on water! Loons do the other dance, the "penguin dance" (right), when people disturb them.

Loons often do the penguin dance to scare enemies away from loon chicks. If boaters do not leave quickly, the loons might dance until they collapse and die.

Loons are excellent fliers, but they are not very good at taking off. They work extra hard to get into the air.

Loons take care of their feathers by *preening*. They use only their bills to keep themselves clean.

After *mating* in spring, male and female loons build a nest to lay their eggs and care for their young. These nests are not very fancy. The loons just pick up pieces of weeds and grass with their bills and plunk them down in a pile along the lake's edge.

The female loon usually lays two olive-brown eggs. This dark color *camouflages* the eggs and makes them difficult for enemies to spot.

Both the male and female loons take turns sitting on the eggs. This keeps the eggs warm so the little chicks inside will grow. Day after day, the loon parents *incubate* the eggs. Then, after about one month, the eggs begin to hatch!

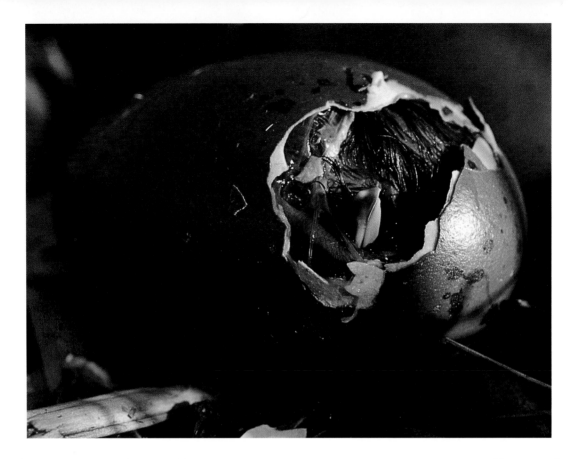

The loon chicks are eager to play!

Because they cannot dive yet, the new chicks depend on their parents to feed them little bits of fish. After a week or so, they begin diving on their own, but it takes a while to learn how to catch the slippery little fish.

Sometimes the water is too cold, so the chicks ride on their parents' backs.

These "free rides" also keep the chicks safe from underwater *predators*.

This little chick is trying to sing like its parents. But the only sound it can make is a peep! The chick will have to grow bigger and stronger before it can sing the loud and thrilling song that makes the loons so magical.

Glossary

adapted — designed or changed over time to move easier and live more comfortably

camouflage — to hide or disguise in order to blend in with the surroundings

incubate — to keep someone or something warm and safe

mate — to join together (animals) to produce young

migrate — to move from one place to another

plumage — a bird's feathers

predator — an animal that hunts other animals for food

preening — cleaning up or smoothing out

prey — an animal hunted or caught for food

Index